Abandon Solitude ~ Love
Book 2

Abandon Solitude ~ Love
Book 2

PUBLISHED BY: Pau Pau
Copyright © 2017

Disclaimer
The information contained in this ebook is for general information purposes only. The information is provided by the authors and while we endeavor to keep the information up to date and correct, we make no representations or warranties of any kind, express or implied, about the completeness, accuracy, reliability, suitability or availability with respect to the ebook or the information, products, services, or related graphics contained in the ebook for any purpose. Any reliance you place on such information is therefore strictly at your own risk.

One day is short, if you are happy, then you will laugh, if you aren't happy, then wait a while and then laugh.

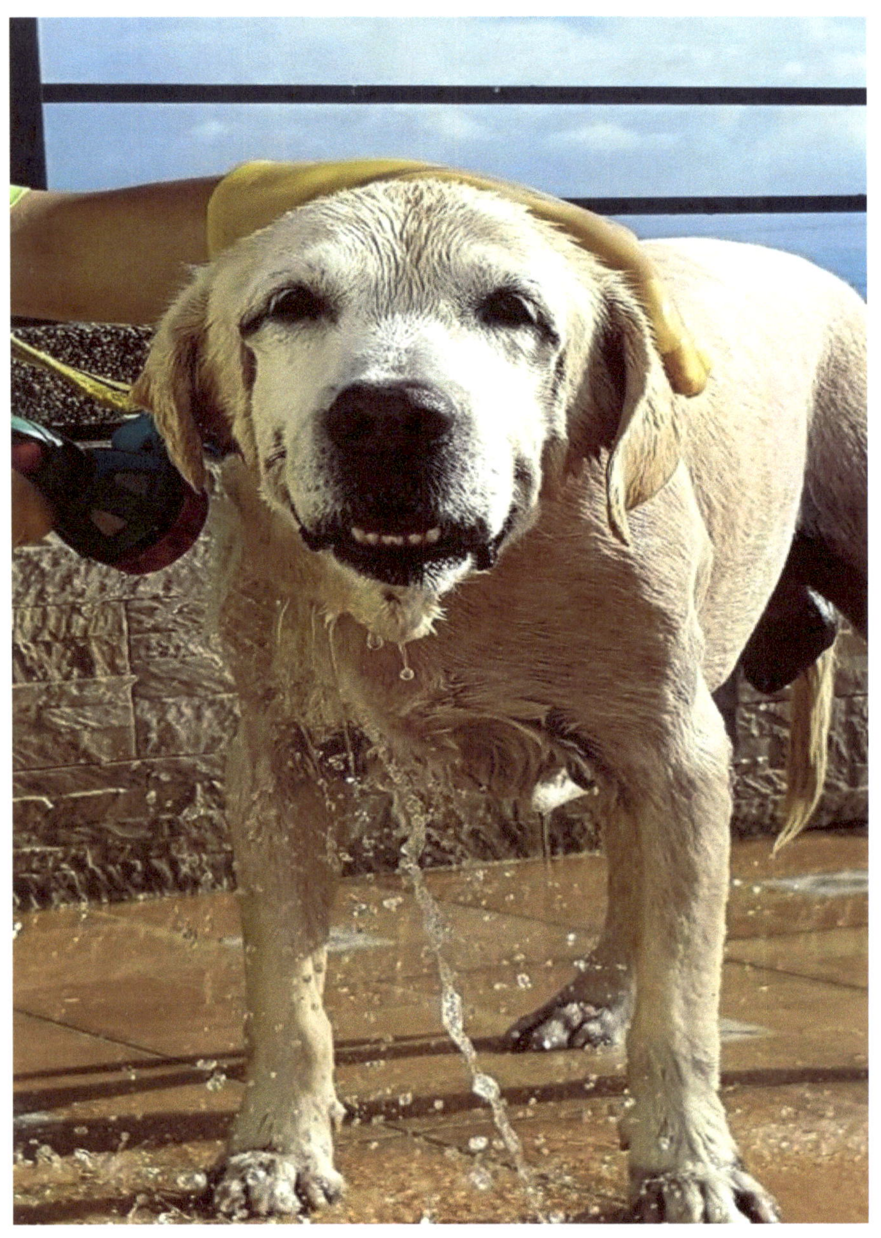

Suddenly looking back, everyone smile disappears right away,
one's use disappears. There is no footprint. No matter what
time,the most important thing is when you start, do not stop. No
matter when once it ends, afterwards, there is no regret in the
heart. All I can do organize my feelings, and move forwards.
A drop of moonlight is like water, touch the eternal flame of the
heart.

In the morning, the sun shone on the grass. I stand hold the windows, the door is low, but the sun is very bright.
The grass is generating seeds, the wind is nightingale the leaves. I stand speechless, but it's perfect

No one can always accompany you unconditionally,
You know, during a rainy day, even the shadow will be absent.

In fact, there aren't many people who are willing to listen to your complaints and who are willing to stand by you during the hard times. Hold it tight when you see one.

Happiness is a song, very quiet.

I am powerful fighter.

This world, there are no accident.

Life has always been very simple, and simple is perfect.

Give yourself a piece of content, give yourself a piece of reality,
give yourself a piece of understanding.
and you will be less confused.

Stand it the spotlight, live the life you want.

Expect yourself: no matter what you do,
Remember to do for yourself,
then there is no complaint.

True love, is not trying to please you,
but once I see you I smile.

Looking back, you cannot hold time back, staring at yourself.
Reflecting, you cannot hold time still.
Therefore, try to smile lightly.

Am ricas

The noise of harvest during winter...... at the end of winter. Express your maturity, in the day of a busy life, change the seasons and fasten your footsteps.
The cold and warm changes in the city's are not obvious. Only in the countrysides will allow you to see the changes.
In the night of the countryside, it will allow you to see the seasonal changes, the sky is so high, so blue, so clear.
Lift your head up....
the smell of the countryside in the winter will allow you to turn brown into green.
The silence of the countryside will give you degrees of loneliness.
From the quietness , there is display of emptiness.
I gave you all I can give,left nothing behind.
Season changing, stars moving, the countryside can repeat the scenery of yesterday.
Show the life of the land, we as human beings cannot bring back what was lost in life.
You can only feel sad about what is gone,life has no emotion!
The dreams of the farmers,
born in the spring,
harvesting in the summer,
locked in the autumn,
Dreams follow each season rhythmically.
And how about us~the people far away from our land?
Dreams will be rooted anywhere in our hearts and grow up little by little .

As long as in your heart there is a dream, ability in your mind, the dream of our life is everywhere
and grows infinitely.
Even if you fail today, translate this as the autumn day of the farmers.
Crossing the night of winter, riding on the road of tomorrow, spring will be there !
The scenery of the seasons will repeat itself. We cannot hold our youth forever.
The farmers dreams should follow the seasons .
Our dreams are rooted in our hearts.
Only hard work can be harvested,
Only paid to have income.
New year approaching
Should not continue to indulge in impetuous, no longer sinking in the torrent of materialism,
Expecting a new life emotion, a new life of thinking.